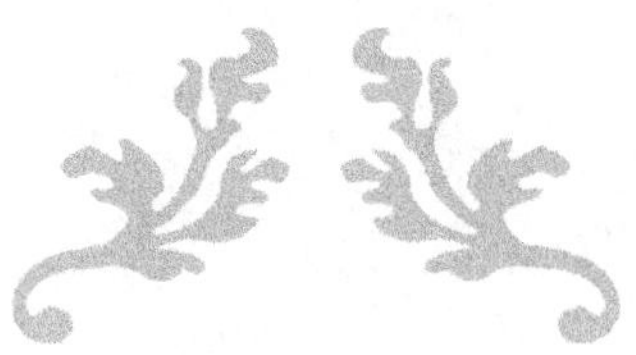

MAKE MONEY ONLINE

A Self-Help Guide To Understanding Ways To Make Good Income Per Month With Your Online Business And Gain Financial Freedom

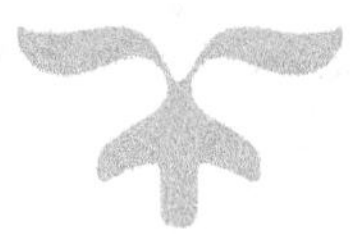

BENJAMIN BLUE

content within this book has been derived from various sources. Please consult a licensed professional before attempting any techniques outlined in this book.

By reading this document, the reader agrees that under no circumstances is the author responsible for any losses, direct or indirect, which are incurred as a result of the use of information contained within this document, including, but not limited to, errors, omissions, or inaccuracies.

Table of Contents

INTRODUCTION

In the world today, it is difficult if not impossible for a business to survive without a social media presence. The simple fact is that you need social media if you are to achieve your business goals as an entrepreneur.

Thanks to the Internet, billions of people around the world can now connect easily, and you can easily gain access to these people as a business owner or entrepreneur.

It doesn't matter if you own a big business or a small one; it certainly doesn't matter if your business is already established or not. Every business needs to include social media as a primary marketing strategy in the business plan in order to ensure success.

Social networking platforms have made it easier for businesses and entrepreneurs to connect with prospects, increase brand awareness, and boost leads and conversions. With billions of people using social media platforms monthly, you have no reason not to tap into the vast pool of opportunities.

A common misconception many entrepreneurs have about social media marketing is that they ought to have a large number of followers before they can utilize social media for marketing.

Social media marketing is not quite like that. The best thing about marketing through social media is that you can start whenever you want. It's possible to start from scratch as long as you develop a niche and create content that solves common consumer problems. In fact, you may even find the whole process enjoyable.

There are several social media sites you can take advantage of as a business owner. But, before we get to discussing them, let's find out the exact reason why social media is such a big deal in business today.

Plenty of benefits abound for businesses that market their products or services through social media. Of all these benefits and advantages, let's check out the 5 most important and indisputable benefits for your business.

CHAPTER 1 STRONG ONLINE PRESENCE

What do people see when they search online for you? Before you can ever speak to anyone of authority online about anything, you must first look like you are someone that is of the caliber to be taken seriously. This initial step is essential to success or failure in the online world.

So, before you even begin setting up profiles, look at the photos of yourself that you're thinking about using. What do they look like?

Were they taken professionally? Are you alone in the photo? Or did you crop your image out of a group shot because you were having a good hair day? Hopefully, it's not your passport, driver's license or school photo that you're thinking of using. Even worse would be to use an image of yourself on vacation, in a T-shirt or swimsuit with a beer in your hand. I'm only mentioning this because I've actually seen that photo on what was supposed to be a professional profile. A casual photo like that should only be used if your business is directly involved in the sale or promotion of everything in the photo

When it's possible to have a well-lit, professional photo taken for a few dollars, no one should ever go without one. This is just too important to be taken lightly.

Think about it! Put yourself on the other side of an online interaction. If you are a busy executive or someone of authority and someone else tries to contact you for advice, direction, a problem with a product they have or a new idea to partner with you on, who are you going to believe more and respond to faster:

Someone who's profile picture is in a T-shirt drinking beer with friends on the deck of a run-down house with a profile that highlights main accomplishments as winning the 3rd-grade kick, pass and punt competition.

Someone dressed in business attire sitting in his or her neat and tidy office with an interesting painting or great view in the background and listing measurable achievements in business for the last ten years.

The answer is pretty obvious. Right? First impressions are everything when it comes to negotiating or asking for anything from anyone. Whether it's an online communication or not, your online presence will come into play at some point in time. And if your profile is not up to snuff, you're just asking to be disappointed and frustrated.

The web is an open book, and anybody can find out anything about anyone at any time, from anywhere in the world. Whether you like it or not, your online first impression is already being made. And there is a chance there is something out there that you may not be aware of. That "something" might not be showing you in the most favorable light. That is why it is imperative to make your image as spotless and believable as possible if you want to be taken seriously.

Think about this: Would you go to a local department store, buy a bunch of big poster boards and fill them with photos of your kids, the names of friends and family, including addresses, where the kids go to school, type of ice cream they like and where they hang out, then hold those posters up in the middle of your town? Would you include on one poster the kind of car you drive, where you go out to

dinner, where you work and what you like to do for fun, when and where you're going on vacation? Would you also take along a bull horn to shout to everyone within earshot "Hey, look at me. Here is all my personal information as well as when I will be out of town and here is a list of all the valuable things I have and who/what is important to me."? Sounds pretty crazy, doesn't it?

I just described the contents of most people's Facebook pages. The only difference is that not just one city block can see it, but the entire world. That's right…THE WHOLE WORLD. So, now that you have broken out into a cold sweat of a reality check, make sure your social presence only shows what you want the world to see.

Not only do you want to protect yourself and your loved ones, in my opinion, the details of our private lives should remain just that— private. As for our public lives in business and such, our online footprints need to be as spotless as possible. Before posting anything, consider how it might impact the person who views it or reads your words—even what you choose to repost. Don't risk offending someone and giving them pause about connecting or doing business with you.

Putting Your Best Foot Forward

If you do not already have an online presence, it's time to fix that. If you do have a website or accounts with various social media platforms, it's time to do some analysis. What I am suggesting is that when you look at your online footprint, make sure you are putting your best foot forward.

Here is a great way to test this. Find five friends or relatives that you trust to give you honest, confidential opinions. Ask them to search for you online. Their goal is to report back their findings, especially anything negative. Make it kind of a game. Remember, pick people you can trust to tell you the truth. You need honesty in case they find something like an inappropriate photo or a comment that might not be well-accepted by the average person. If possible, ask an old friend, a newer friend, and possibly a relative so they'll each have

different thoughts about what and where to search when it comes to you. Have them email the results to you with links to what they find.

By doing this, you are seeing first-hand what anyone else could find if they were to search your name in your town or within your industry. Hopefully, there will not be any mug shots or line ups with you in them! If there are, you have more work to do than is covered in this book. Let's hope there are no unpleasant surprises of any kind. On a positive note, they may find good news about you that you may have forgotten and could find beneficial in your current job or job search.

Once you take a look at their findings and verify that what they found is about you and not someone else with the same name, it's decision time. What will you do with this information? Reference as much of the "good stuff" that is pertinent to the persona you would like employers, clients or potential clients to know. Again, unless you coach Pop Warner football, you can leave out the news item about winning the 3rd-grade kick, pass and punt competition. If you find yourself lacking in positive information about your skills or experience, it will be time to reach out to those you've successfully worked with to gather some recommendations. In the online world, the rule is to squelch the negative and promote the positive.

Reputation Management

Let's say your friendly researchers found some dirt on you. Perhaps there's a relationship or an incident in your past that shows you in a less-than-professional light. It's time to take some steps toward reputation management.

If the information is posted on your own site or social media platform, remove it immediately. If others have shared something like a drunken-dance photo that embarrasses you, ask them to remove it. If they truly care about you, they'll want what's best for you. Once you explain how you're working to build your online reputation, most people will understand. If your embarrassing moment, whatever it is, has been shared out in cyberspace, beyond your control, it can be challenging to get rid of it. However, there are ways of pushing it down in search engines so others who are doing cursory research on you won't be likely to find it.

Several years ago, I saw a good friend who owned a business getting into a little trouble with the law. He ended up under house arrest for over a year while awaiting trial. Not only was this inconvenient for the running of his business, but it was also a matter of public record so anyone could find out about it. The facts of the matter were that he was framed by a city official. When he went to trial, he had to pay a stiff fine and was set free. However, the online damage was done.

When you searched for him online, the first 20 listings on Google showed articles about his arrest and confinement while awaiting trial. The result of him being framed and later set free wasn't as easy to find.

Since I have a web development company, he asked if I could help him eliminate the bad press. Though we couldn't get it removed from the web, we were able to move it down further in search results. Search engines use popularity, relevance and timeliness as some of the main criteria to rank posts. We began by analyzing what was there and then posting more relevant and timely information about the guy. There were several steps involved and it took some time, but eventually, the bad press moved deeper and deeper into the web. The positive information we posted appeared first.

There are other strategies to help push negative information down the line.

In the case of my friend, he was not a member of any social media platform at the time. We were able to develop some nice, clean, professional profiles for him on Facebook, LinkedIn, Twitter and YouTube. These profiles went a long way toward getting him positively portrayed in Google searches for his name.

Note: If you have a common name, know that others with your same name will have both positive and negative information show up. Anyway, you can honestly differentiate yourself will help. Instead of posting as John Smith, consider adding your middle initial, your industry, or city prominently in your profiles. An example that

comes to mind on LinkedIn is for the sales trainer, Tom Hopkins with whom I co-authored a book. A search for his name brings up several listings. Since his name is rather common, he uses "Tom Hopkins Sales Trainer."

Another strategy to consider is to buy your name as a domain and create a personal website. Again, with a common name, this could require some creativity. If you have an unusual name or nickname, you may want to use that if it's available. Having a personal website with your name as the domain will not only help with reputation management, it will also make it easier for people to find the information you want them to find when they search for you.

Invest time in learning about keywords and phrases. When you optimize your site with the keywords people will use to search for you, it's more likely they'll get the result you want—your site. If there's anything negative about you that's still out there, use some of the keywords from those negative postings on your site as well. Those keywords will cause the site you control to pop up in the results.

Another way to create positive search results for your name or your company name is to write a blog. Write briefly about interesting information regarding your industry or profession. You may also want to write about your experiences and aspirations. With the blog, you would again use the keywords people will use to search for you—both the positive ones and negative ones.

From what I've found, WordPress, Blogger and Blogspot seem to be popular programs for a simple blog. They offer some very professional-looking themes. They also have some simple plugins that make it easy to optimize your posts. Those plugins coach you into improving blog post titles and keywords. You can also imbed photos and videos into your posts, making them more appealing to your visitors.

When you write your copy for the blog posts, consider referencing other known sources within your industry or topic. Including links to those sources will help build the relevance of your blog and increase your odds of improving your Google ranking.

CHAPTER 2 BUILDING A PERSONAL BRAND

A brand is not a product or a service. It is an idea, a design, a symbol, a behavior and a reputation. For example, both Samsung and Apple operate in the same space of technology, but they represent technology in totally different ways. That is their brand. A brand is a distinction between what one thing is and not the other. That is what makes each one unique. In simple words, you have a few things that others have and a few things that others do not have. That is your USP and your differentiator. That will make your personal brand!

So, we all carry our personal brand. All your life, you have shared your brand with everyone you met or interacted with. How you portray yourself defines what your brand is. But do you believe that this represents you in a complete, real sense?

What Is Personal Branding?

Personal branding is similar to the branding of a product or service. However, in the case of personal branding, this product or service is an individual.

Personal Branding is a practice of marketing yourself to a specific audience of people. It is about promoting your skills, ideas & experiences to people who are interested in what you have to offer. Let us begin with your name. That is your brand. How your appearance distinguishes you from others, is your brand design. You have different parents, values, personality, perception and qualities from others. All these make you unique.

In essence, personal branding is all about being your authentic self.

For example, you might be fantastic at putting outfits and accessories together, which people find attractive. So, with time, you gain followers on social media who appreciate your sense of styling and deem you as a style inspiration. Similarly, you might be great at online gaming, and you share tips and tricks regarding that on social media. Gradually, you gain a following of people who are interested in gaming.

Make sense?

CVs or resumes are no longer enough. In the future, they will exist only as fossils. What will thrive is your unique promise. Your brand. Anyone can have a similar set of skills and qualifications as yours, and so, they can poach your opportunities. To win, you need to be indispensable. You have to be not just the right fit, but the only fit for a job. Regardless of whether you wish to pursue a career or become an influencer, it would be best if you had your brand to sell your skills.

Here are the steps to create your personal brand: Step 1: Know your strengths

Step 2: Know your shortcomings Step 3: Know your values
Step 4: Identify your passion Step 5: Find your niche
Step 6: Position yourself appropriately Step 7: Understand your competition Step 1: Knowing Your Strengths
Your strengths are an essential factor in creating your personal brand. It does not depend on what you think your strengths are, but on what others believe are your strong areas.
Think of people who you feel have a fabulous personal brand. You will observe that these people have complete clarity on what they want in life and who they are at their core. They know their unique

selling points and what value they bring to the table. After doing the following exercise, you will join their league too. So, let us begin.

Write down the following in a notebook to identify your strengths: Your career highlights

Professional moments or incidents that you are proud of 2-3 most fulfilling projects of yours

Think of why you felt fulfilled while executing them or when they were done

The role you usually play in a group project Perception of your group members about you

Your techniques and thought process to overcome challenges and obstacles

Tools that you use often

Professional or personal things that bring you joy, something you enjoy getting involved in

Things you like to discuss and debate about

Now, describe each of your strengths in just one word. Write those down too.

Pick individuals who know you, your partner, family, colleagues and friends and ask them to share their understanding of your strengths. In the wake of doing that contrast your rundowns and theirs. Show them your list and check whether they see you in the same light as you see yourself.

It might seem obvious; however, you would be astounded by the number of people who would list down all that they have ever done. Pass on your energy and connect your strengths to gauge results. Tell your target audience about your gifts. Convey it to them adequately utilizing all resources accessible to you. While interacting with your audience, recall your qualities and morals. That will set you apart.

Step 2: Knowing Your Shortcomings

We all have certain shortcomings and acknowledging them is never easy. However, we do not wish to live a life full of disappointments. Therefore, you and we need to be honest about our shortcomings. Remember that weakness is anything from being utterly uninterested about anything in life to have limited skills to do anything of interest.

Let us do a similar activity as we did for strengths to identify your weak areas:

List down the things about your education and career that you do not like at all

Note down the reasons why you dislike those aspects

Think hard about your beliefs on how worthy you are and if you deserve better

Ask yourself if you feel drained merely by the thought of performing specific tasks

List down such tasks that make you feel out of action

Make a list of all the low points of your career

Write reasons against each on why you think that they were the low points

If you are given a group task, which role would you never like to perform, and why?

Have there been any tasks that you have done, but that did not bring you any joy?

Did these tasks fail? Why was that?

Do you ever give up? What makes you do that?

In a conversation, at what point do you feel uninspired to talk more?

Are there any particular topics that you feel uncomfortable talking about?

List down 10 of your weaknesses.

Be honest with yourself. Know that there is no need to waste time on shortcomings that do not hamper your professional growth. Now, establish what limitations you can turn into strengths to kick-start your career. Start learning the skills to propel your growth. If talking to people makes you nervous, become a regular at networking events and work on yourself bit by bit.

Step 3: Knowing Your Values

Do you have some principles, a code that you use to navigate through life? Those principles form your value system. They determine your moral compass, your personality, attitude, actions, reactions, and so on. Do not confuse them with your profession.

Take five minutes to visualize these people and think about what their personal brand is – what do they stand for. Understand the difference between their profession and their brand.

Barack Obama Marie Kondo Pele

Music band, Queen Mark Manson

Seth Godin Oprah Winfrey Meryl Streep Anna Winton Frida Kahlo

Picture it like this: Perhaps your reason for unhappiness at work is that your work is not aligned with the values you uphold. Having values, therefore, is taking a stand for your beliefs. It is critical to align what you engage yourself in with who you are at your core.

By knowing your values, you get an understanding of who you are and what you stand for. To establish and route your thoughts in a way that matches your passion, you need to have strong values. Simply put, before involving yourself in anything, ask yourself, "Is this in sync with my values and what I stand for?"

Step 4: Identifying Your Passion

Have a passion for what you do! That is the biggest secret. It might seem difficult to reconcile the idea of passion and work. But it is not impossible. Clubbing your passion and work will bring you more joy than you can ever imagine. It will keep you inspired and wanting more. That is why influencers are flourishing. They did not take the beaten path or picked a career because many people were making easy money out of it. They picked it because they felt passionate about it and turned it into a viable business model. With passion, you can do that too!

If you still cannot put the finger on your passion, recall a time when you found it challenging to wait to do something. Rewind to the day when you jumped out of your bed in the morning. Think of the things that broke you into tears of joy. Do not forget the projects that unleashed your creativity and filled your head with ideas. See, it

is all about feeling stimulated and motivated to do something. That something is your passion!

Ask yourself:

What do I like about my current job?

If I were to volunteer, which charity would you choose? Why? How do most of your days go and in doing what?

Now take a minute to think about the potential influencers you follow on Instagram. As you do that, answer the following questions in your head:

What do I love about my current job?

Which would the charity of my choice if I were to volunteer in the future? Why?

What do I spend most of my time doing?

The chances are you follow certain influencers because they create valuable content in your areas of interest. These areas of interest are also called "niches".

Step 5: Finding Your Niche

The following exercise will help you understand more about what your niche could be and how you can start to build the foundations of your brand. Be as specific as you can when answering the questions below. You will need this information later down the line.

Who are you? (Write a short paragraph.) What makes you unique?

List all of your passions (Don't just list things you are "kind of interested in", but the things you are genuinely passionate about.)

What are you good at? (The skills that distinguish you from your friends and family? It can be anything. It might help to think about what people compliment you on and what do you get attention for)

Based on the above information, who could your audience be? (To make it easier, make a list starting with "people who are interested in".

Now you have a list of "niches" that you could become a mega influencer in before we get into the techniques needed to grow a huge following.

Step 6: Positioning Yourself

Once you are crystal clear about your values, strengths, attributes, niche, and passion, it is time to now position yourself. What does that mean exactly? It means that you establish how you would like others to see you based on your qualities, strengths, values, attributes, and passion. Do not forget – it is all about authenticity. No matter where you work, you must be consistent about who you say you are.

So, create a positioning statement for yourself. Pin it on a board. You can use this statement during interviews too. It is not going to be about a boring career summary, but a powerful and fresh take on where you see yourself. It will capture your essence and uniqueness.

Step 7: Understanding Your Competition

Make a list of ten mega influencers in any particular niche or industry. Take a look at how they present their accounts and the kind of content they are posting. What times are they posting? How many times do they update their content? How are they interacting with their followers? How many social media platforms are they present? Is there content same everywhere or are they creating and posting different content everywhere? If yes, what are the key differences, and how do they help these influencers?

Do not try to memorize it. Chart it. Yes, create a chart of influencers who you envy or find irresistible. Use the following pointers to fill in the chart against the name of each. Do not slack here as the chart you create now will come in handy when you create a killer content campaign for your brand

Account Name: Are the account name and handle different?

Niche: Do they operate in multiple niches? What is the ratio?

Display Picture: Is it a logo or a picture? Is it generic or a decent shot?

Bio: Add a summary of what the account bio states.

Call to Action (or CTA for short): Simply put, does the bio direct followers to do something specific? For example, does it ask them to click follow? Visit a website?

Content-Type: Does the account have videos, images or both? What does the account have more of?

The theme of the content: What kind of images/videos is the account sharing with its followers? Is it short "humor" videos? Amazing landscape images? Selfies of the account owner? Product images?

Followers: How many followers does the account have? How many are they following?

Engagement: Engagement means the number of likes, views, and comments each post is receiving. Look at the last 3 - 5 posts on each account and note these down. The more likes and comments show what your audience is reacting strongly to.

Posting schedule: How often is the account posting? Is it once per day? Three times per day? 6 times per day?

Seeing what successful accounts are doing is one of the most effective ways to grow your personal brand account.

32

CHAPTER 3 FINDING THE RIGHT NICHE

When it comes to marketing the content that you create as effectively as possible, the first, and perhaps the most important thing that you will need to consider is which niche of the market you are going to cater to. For example, the online dating market is a broad category that holds several different niches including things like polyamory, green dating, sacred sexuality, soul mates and more. These niches can then be broken down even further into things such as polyamory over 40 or homosexual sacred sexuality.

While hosting a website that purely functioned as an aggregation of content related to a specific niche was once very common, Google has since changed the way it ranks websites which means that if you aim for something along these lines then you aren't ever going to receive any search engine ranking traffic. This means that in order to be successful when it comes to affiliate marketing you are going to need to market yourself as much as the products or services you are advertising if you hope to make a profit in the long run.

Remember, affiliate marketing is a slow and steady process of amassing users and teaching them that they can trust you which means that it is crucial to pick a niche that you can stick with for more than a few months. This is why hobbies and interests are such a natural fit if you already spend hours each week obsessing over something, taking the next step into writing about products other people in your situation would care about is a natural step.

If, as you take stock of your hobbies and interests, you don't find anything that obviously sticks out as a potential affiliate marketing revenue stream, chances are you are taking too much of a macro look at your life. If this is the case, you will instead want to map out your daily routine with an eye towards the things that are popular enough to have a built-in audience that is interested in them, while at the same time not being so broadly popular that finding space in the niche would be difficult.

After you have between five and 10 potential topics in mind, the next thing you are going to want to do is to break them down into more specific categories, two or three per topic should do it, and then do a little extra online research to see how the space is currently defined by your future competition in the space. You don't need to focus on coming up with only profitable ideas at this step, only a wide variety of options. The goal is to get the creative juices flowing and help you tap into some sub-niches that you may otherwise miss.

If, despite your best efforts, you can't come up with anything that really seems to stick, but you do have an idea of the types of products you are interested in marketing, then you should head to These products will all be classified into categories which might put you on the right track towards possible sub-niches and niches.

Narrow Down Your List

Locate the right target audience: After you have brainstormed a number of potential target niches, the next thing you will want to do is to cut them down to the best of the best when it comes to speaking to the types of customers you are going to want to target. Finding the right audience can be done in numerous different ways, starting with a consideration of your own demographic and the people like you who might be interested in the products you want to advertise.

Like the niche you choose, it is important to focus on a very specific segment of the market as every group is going to have very different likes and dislikes that influence their buying habits. For example, if you decide to focus only on men, then you will find some broad similarities, but a 19-year-old college student is going to be radically different in terms of their priorities when compared to a man of 40 who is married with two children. This goes to show that if your target audience is too broad you will only end up appealing to no one.

Consider their problems: Once you have landed on a specific demographic, the next thing you will need to consider is the types of

problems that the demographic ends up facing on a regular basis. Furthermore, you will want to keep in mind things such as their desires and aspirations, as well as the issues they might routinely run into when it comes to following their dreams. Once you have done some brainstorming, the next thing you will want to do is to head back to Google and plug in the words you have come up with to see what the general online space regarding them looks like. If the problems, you come up with don't see many results then it isn't really a problem your target audience is concerned with.

Consider the potential for profit: After you have landed on multiple different problems that you know your target audience needs to solve, you will then need to consider if there are products out there that this group would be interested in paying for in order to solve them. This is an especially important step as there is no point in creating advertising content if your target audience is unlikely to bite on the solutions you are peddling. If you like the audience you have chosen, and then it is best to focus on items that are well within their price range, though not so cheap that they would constitute an impulse buy. This will ensure they don't spend too long thinking about each decision, while at the same time ensuring they still seek some guidance.

This will allow you to view search results as they are filtered by keyword as a means of determining how frequently they come in search results in general. It will also show you the breakdown of the timeline of the searches, allowing you to determine if the products you are considering selling are on the rise or on the way out of the public consciousness.

With these details in mind, you will then want to visit numerous different existing sites that are doing what you are considering doing to determine what the demand for this type of information currently is. While visiting the competition, it is important to keep an eye out for those that have active advertising beyond Google AdSense as this is a sign that they are popular enough to attract outside advertisers as well. This is a strong sign that there is money to be made from the community you are considering targeting.

Look beyond the obvious: Beyond just understanding the problems that your target audience is going to face on a regular basis, you will also need to consider the ways in which they work to solve these problems themselves. For example, if you are looking to target individuals who are looking for soul mates then you are going to want to consider what exactly that phrase means to them, the qualities that they look for in a romantic partner and even how they approach the idea of love in general.

Considering the potential psyche and deeper motivations of your target audience are going to help you to learn to think as they do which is crucial when it comes to creating the type of content that they legitimately respond to and will hopefully seek out more of.

Only by understanding them both inside and out will you ever be able to realistically create the type of content that really speaks to them in such a way that it generates the types of results they are looking for.

Decide if you can stick with it: Once you have found a niche that seems as though it is going to work for you, the next step is to have an honest conversation with yourself regarding your ability to stick with the niche and provide useful, and profitable contents in the long-term. This means more than creating the stray bit of content here and there, if you want to make a true profit with affiliate marketing you are going to need to create a public persona that those in the niche respond to. This is the only way to build their trust and create the type of traffic to your site in the long-term that you are going to need to generate a reliable passive income stream.

Consider industry trends: Just because a specific niche has a strong audience at the moment, doesn't mean that you can jump in with both feet without doing some research first. This is because it is quite possible that the niche you have found has already peaked when it comes to popularity. If this is the case then, despite your best efforts, you will only ever see diminishing returns which means it is best to start somewhere else instead to avoid having to start from square one again in a matter of months.

The trending tool from Google is extremely useful in this instance as it shows how often a keyword was searched in a given month.

Specifically, in this instance, you are going to want to target niches where the number of searches is each monthly is always on the rise as opposed to those where the biggest surge of search popularity has already peaked.

Find an entry point: After you have found a few promising niches, the next thing you will want to do is to determine if there is still enough room in the niche for you and your unique spin on things. Once more you will want to visit Google and do a simple search utilizing the types of keywords that your target audience is likely going to use. The types of results that are going to be the most useful are going to feature a wide variety of sites, with no site being listed more than once on the first page. The less diverse the first page of Google search results, the more difficult it will be for you to make a dent in the competition. If there are four or fewer sites on the first page, then you are going to want to look elsewhere as the odds are stacked against you.

Consider your ability to generate content: Assuming you have come across a niche or sub-niche that you believe looks promising, the next thing you are going to need to do is to consider if you have the ability to create enough content to get your site up and running. To start, you are going to want to come up with at least 50 ideas for topics that you will be able to create content around, as well as 25 ideas for smaller social media posts to keep the stream of new users flowing in while you are working on generating more substantial content.

When you first get started you are going to want to post around 3 different pieces of content a week so the 50 that you come up with to start should be enough to get you through the first month. Instead, you should focus on creating two pieces of content that relate to the niche in question for each one piece of advertising content you create.

Once you have built up your archives a bit, you can slow down somewhat, though slowing down too much will curtail much of your existing hard work. Ideally, you will never want to post less than two pieces of new content per week to keep users visiting your site on a regular basis. If you can brainstorm the required amount of

content after a day or two of doing research and considering the topic from all sides, then you may want to go back to the drawing board and pick something more personal to try again as this is a sure sign that you are going to continue having trouble moving forward. While you might not like the idea of starting from scratch this far in, it is going to be far preferable to moving ahead with a half-baked idea and ending up back at square one after months of effort.

Popular Niche Ideas

While certain topics are going to be a flash in the pan, starting off strong before fizzling out sooner than later, others are going to be evergreen and will always have a target audience waiting to consume new content. For the best results, start with one of these and then look for a relatively new sub-niche that you can really put your mark on.

Wealth, health and romance: Known in the content marketing world as the big 3, wealth, health and romance niches are always popular and new sub-niches are always popping up to give them a boost as well. What's more, the target audience for each has long been trained to always be on the lookout for the next big thing which means you will have a group of individuals who are eager to throw money at your product or service. Essentially this means that there are potential customers beyond count out there that are just waiting for someone new (you and your content) to tell them how to solve all their problems and they are willing to throw as much money at the issue as it takes to find the happiness they are looking for.

The health niche is a veritable smorgasbord of sub-niches, from everything to smoking cessation to weight loss trends to help with vanity issues such as hair loss. This is to say nothing of medical conditions for which there is no cure, such as IBS. The wealth niche is useful as it includes a variety of sub-niches that are evergreen including anything to do with passive income, internet marketing, gambling or investing.

Expensive hobbies: When it comes to affiliate marketing, if you can find your own space in the market, there is no better niche than one

that has to do with an expensive hobby. You will never lack for content as new products are always being released, and the target audience you are speaking to is one that is already in the habit of buying new products to support their habit as well. From drone racing to marijuana, if you can put a unique spin on one of these niches you can practically guarantee that if you do the work you can find an audience that is looking to spend money. This is also a good option if you are having a hard time coming up with contents on your own as there will always be plenty of topics surrounding these hobbies to choose from.

Then you should download Word Press. You simply click Install Word Press, enter your space name, and you are a great idea to go. So, to clear up, Blue host is you're facilitating for your site. Word Press is the place you will alter and post every one of your articles. We will presently be choosing a topic for your blog. For your site to be fruitful and get a huge amount of traffic, you will require an incredible subject. Presently, the most extraordinary ones are not free. Which means you may need to put in some cash on it?

Simply realize that you can begin your blog with a free subject, however, the sooner you get a paid topic, the better. You can discover topics on Blue host, Word Press, and numerous different sites. You can without much of a stretch include it to your site.

Ensure whatever subject you pick, it ought to have a perfect design and should be effectively gotten to by the peruses.

44

CHAPTER 4 DAY TRADING

All over the world, stock markets open in the morning. Those day traders who think they can start trading, munching on their breakfast, with no preparation, are among those who make losses. All businesses open in the morning. No successful businessman just gets up, yawns and starts his business activities. Successful professionals arrive in their office with a clear idea of how they will tackle the work and related challenges.

Likewise, to succeed in day trading, one must prepare beforehand. These preparations include many aspects; such as mental, physical, emotional, and financial.

Professional traders have clear advice for day traders; never trade if you are tired or stressed; never trade if you are feeling highly emotional, and trade with clear money management concepts. Day trading is a sophisticated business activity, where people try to earn money by using their intelligence. Therefore, physical or emotional stress can cause harm to your trading business. You will not be able to make rational decisions if you are tired or feeling stressed.

Before you start the day's trading, you should be physically, mentally and emotionally alert. A good night's sleep is necessary for traders to tackle the roller coaster ride of stock markets. Here are a few steps that will help you prepare for day trading with a cool temperament and calm mind.

Before going to sleep, keep your trading plan ready. Note down the important support and resistance levels. Then mentally go over this chart and imagine how you will trade in the next session, in different trend conditions.

Do not spend too much time watching news about stock markets or anything else. Watching the news may create doubts in your mind about stock trends and influence your decision-making power for the next session. If possible, do some breathing exercises on meditation before going to sleep, which will sharpen your focusing power and reduce stress.

Also, prepare your money-plans for the next trading session. How much you will invest? What will be your loss tolerance level? And, what will be your profit booking point? During the trading hours, these decisions have to be taken in a split second, and if you are already prepared, you will not hesitate to take the right decision. These will also help you set your goals for intraday trading. Just stick to your goals and you will not face any decision-making problems during the trading hours.

The final stage of your preparation will be an hour before the markets open in the morning. This is the time when you check the news reports about the business and financial world, and the economic calendar. By doing so, you will know what events could influence that day's trading pattern in the stock market. You can also check how the world markets are trading in that session. Sometimes all markets trade in one direction, which will be beneficial to know before your local stock markets open.

Planning for Trading

In day trading, financial instruments are bought and sold within the same session. Sometimes more than once through the same day. To be successful in this endeavor, traders need to know where the price might make important moves. Technical charts are very helpful tools in deciphering this price moment. Anybody involved in stock trading relies heavily on stock charts, which is why successful traders always create their trading plans before taking any trading decisions.

When you create a trading plan, you are creating an 'assistant' to help you during the trading hours. This assistant will have all the information you will need for day trading; such as trade entry, trade exit, profit booking, stop loss and major price moments. Nobody goes looking for a treasure trove without any map. Likewise; no trader worth his or her salt will trade without a trading plan. Let us look at how a trading plan is created:

A trading plan is based on research, takes time, but saves a lot of effort and precious money during the trading hours. It is one of the most essential tools required for success in day trading. Every day trader has heard this saying 'fail to plan, and plan to fail'. Professional traders don't tire of emphasizing the importance of a trading plan. If you take their advice and prepare a trading plan before the markets open, you are halfway through to successful trading.

A trading plan is prepared before markets open and so, it is open to revisions and changes after markets start to trade and price changes. Every trader has a different trading style and based on that his trading plan could differ from others. But every trading plan must have a few essential details. These are:

1.   Major support and resistance levels: One must mark the major support and resistance levels on the trading chart because these will symbolize the trade entry and exit points. These levels should be visible on charts to help in decision making during the chaotic trading hours.

2. Trade entry rules: Your trading plan should include when and why

you will enter a trade. This could be a detailed explanation like 'if the price goes above X level, then buy'. Or it could be just a green arrow pointing to that price level.

3. Trade exit rules: Like the trade entry point, mark a trade exit or profit booking points on your trading plan. You must follow these rules meticulously, otherwise, these will become useless, if you plan and do not follow them.

4. Money management rules: Some traders like to note down on their trading plan, how much money they will invest in the next session. They keep checking their profits and losses through the session, and if the day's loss reaches its threshold; they stop trading. This is a good example of money-discipline while trading because, in the excitement of trading, one can lose sight of what is happening with the investment capital.

These are the most basic rules to include in the trading plan. As you gain experience and get a hold of trading patterns in stock markets, you can expand your trading plans and include more trading rules in it. But always remember, these rules must be followed. A trading plan is based on research about markets, so every rule is important. Breaking any rule will be like going against the market, which is always harmful to any trader.

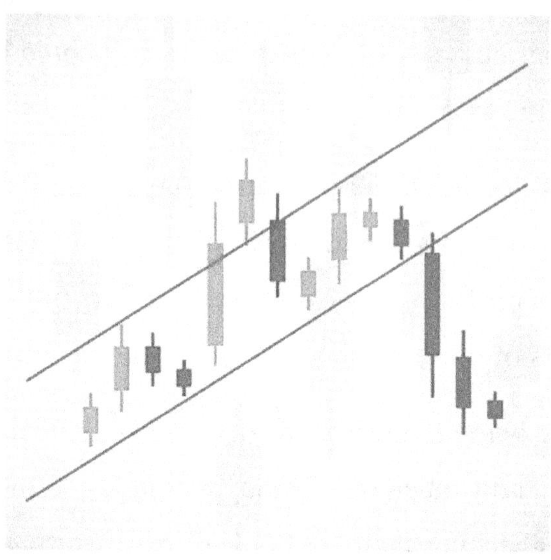

Day traders use different charts for technical analysis. The main types are line charts, bar charts, and candlestick charts. Some Forex traders also use Heiken Ashi and Ranko charts, but candlestick charts remain the most favorite of traders. The reason for this popularity is its simplicity. A green candlestick shows a positive price movement, and a red candlestick signals a fall in price. Day traders use various candlestick patterns to decipher the market trend.

The candlestick charts are more than a hundred years old. These were first used by Japanese rice traders to document the rise and fall in the rice prices. It was such an accurate system that stock traders also adopted it and it has since been a popular chart creating tool.

A single candlestick has two main parts; a body and a tail or wick. The body of the candlestick shows the opening and closing levels, while the wick shows the high and low marks. A green body shows that the price opened low but closed higher. And a red body shows higher open, but lower closing in that time frame. A single candlestick can be assigned to different time frames, ranging from one second to one month. These candlesticks make various patterns

on charts. Traders try to decipher the price moment by how long the wick, or the body is, and how every candlestick is placed with other nearby candlesticks.

Candlestick charts are also used for automatic or algorithm trading, where buy and sell signals are generated by various patterns formed by candlesticks.

The up and down movement in stock prices creates candlesticks on charts. Sometimes, a single candlestick can indicate a trend reversal from high to low or low to high. These are called engulfing candlesticks and are so large that they completely engulf the past candlestick. These can be both bullish and bearish candlesticks. Bullish candlestick is formed when the price-move creates a big positive or green candlestick, which overshadows the past one. It signals that the price is ready to move higher and to start an uptrend.

Its opposite is a bearish engulfing candlestick pattern. Here, the stock price makes a big red candlestick overshadowing the past one. This signals big selling pressure and shows that the price will fall further.

Another popular form of a candlestick is "Doji". Usually, this candlestick forms near the top or the bottom, after the price has made a long moment in either direction. In a Doji candlestick, the body is tiny, and the wicks are long. A small body denotes uncertainty in buyers and sellers; which shows that the market cannot decide whether to go up or down. Such an uncertain signal on top may indicate a trend reversal, and traders prepare for a fall in the market. A Doji formation at the bottom signals that the downtrend may come to an end and traders look for confirmation of a price-rise from lower levels.

Candlesticks create many types of patterns on a technical chart. This could involve a single or two or more candlesticks. There are many books about candlesticks and how to read candlestick charts. Traders who wish to know more about these charts, can read some of those books and enhance their knowledge.

Manage Your Time Effectively

Day trading is a demanding profession and requires significant time. Any market session runs for at least 6 hours a day, and you will have to spend that much time watching and observing markets; even if not reading. Apart from trading hours, a day trader needs to research, create trading plans, and keep learning new things. All these require time and effort.

Therefore; to succeed in day trading, you will need to manage your time effectively. Usually, people want to adopt a day trading career so they will have working flexibility. This means freedom from getting up early and rushing to get caught in the morning traffic. Freedom from having a boss, and of course, financial freedom. Nothing comes easy in this world. A dream life also requires putting in lots of effort. Many day traders find it difficult to complete their trading routines; such as after-hours research and planning. Part- time traders who are already busy with some other work also struggle to prepare for day trading in their spare time.

With just a few adjustments, a day trader can find enough time to complete all steps required for a successful day trading. Here are a few things you will find helpful in managing your time effectively, while day trading:

1. Healthy sleeping hours: day trading can be a mentally exhausting activity. Watching the computer screen for 6 hours a day, then reading news reports, preparing charts- all these tires our brains and eyes. This is the reason day traders must have at least 6 hours of sleep during the weekdays. TV watching or being glued to your smartphone can increase stress on your eyes and make you feel more strained. For a successful career in day trading, you should sacrifice these low-value activities.

2. Fix targets: the human brain is most active when it is given a target to achieve. So, create reasonable monthly or weekly targets in your

day trading. Challenge yourself to achieve these goals with self-discipline. For example, set a target of trading only twice in a session,

for a week. This will be an indirect way of managing your money and reducing the risk of over-trading.

3. Prioritize your tasks: fix times for different tasks such as trade planning, charting and going through the economic data and news. For day trading, you need to do all these activities regularly. Assign time and prioritize which one is the most important and do that activity first. For example, trade planning is the most essential tool for successful day trading but reading news items are not that important. So, give priority to planning your trades first.

4. Relax: It is of utmost importance that day traders relax over the weekend when markets are closed. Some traders keep going over news reports, chatting in forums about what will happen in the markets next week. However; it is essential to take time off from trading and relax. Day trading is a stressful vocation and too much stress can burn anyone out. Shut down your computers once market close for the day and relax for an hour or two before picking up your trade planning activities. Likewise, over the weekend, when markets are closed for two days, it is essential that one unwinds and enjoys the free time away from markets and trading.

Believe it or not, the biggest stumbling block for day traders is the beginning. They jump into stock markets and start trading heavily, thinking of making big money instantly. This is their first and the costliest mistake. The functioning of stock markets is always very chaotic.

From a calm morning, the opening of the stock markets is like rushing into the path of an Express train. When stock markets open for trade, day traders have to make split-second decisions, monitor the technical signals, keep an eye on the price movement, think one step ahead of markets, and take care of trade entry and exit points. All of these things happen together. In such situations, it is difficult

for day traders, especially beginners, to make mistakes. Therefore, day traders should initially keep their trading restricted. They should focus only on one or two stocks, and trade only once or twice through a single day.

Starting small is also important for your risk and reward ratio management. Even if you stumble in the earlier stages of your career, you will keep the losses to a minimum by trading less. Day trading is like learning to ride a bicycle where initially you will often fall. But once you get used to it, you will learn how to balance it. In day trading also, it is advisable to watch and observe stock markets for the first few days. Prepare your trading plans, then watch how the price moves with the signals. Slowly you will start getting the hang of the seemingly chaotic behavior of stock markets, and a definite pattern will start to emerge. This pattern will show you where to start your trading and where to exit.

Many brokers have now started giving facility of margin trading, where day traders can trade with a fraction of the required money. For example, if Apple shares are trading at $200, day traders are given the margin facility of trading it for a smaller margin of, say, $20. On the surface, it is a win-win situation for the broker and the client. It increases the business for the broker; and gives day traders facility to invest very little money for trading. But the margin facility can also become a trap for day traders by encouraging them to trade more. It gives them a false sense of having more money to trade. That's why intraday traders must make a rule of trading only once or twice in the initial days and stick to this rule.

Apart from the invested money and the number of trades; day traders should also keep their profit target small. It is easy to make profits if markets are in a big trend. Then day traders start dreaming of making millions every day. This makes them greedy and they invest more and more money; trade many times a day; hope to catch a trend again. In stock markets that does not happen often, and they end up losing money instead of making profits. Always keep your profit targets small and achievable. Accumulate your profits, which will become big over a period

Like any other business, day trading also needs careful money management. As a day trader, you will invest a certain capital for trading, and you must keep track of profit and losses. You should always know how your business is doing. You cannot keep on investing money, hoping to become profitable someday.

The first step in money management during day trading is, decide how much you are going to invest in every single trade. After that, decide what will your stop loss. This means, at what level of loss you will exit that trade. Before trading, you must make a mental note of how many trades you will do it that session and keep that number to a minimum. Fix how much loss you will allow on all your trades in that session. For example, if you are thinking of doing two trades that day, and you can tolerate $10 loss for each of those, you should stop trading once your loss reaches $20. Such discipline in trading is crucial if you don't want to run out of your investment money within a few days of trading. This is not pessimistic thinking that all your trades will make losses, but a prudent money management skill, where you decide the limit of the loss you will tolerate.

CHAPTER 5 MANAGING RISK IN DAY TRADING

Three Steps in Managing Risks

Here are the three steps you can take to effectively manage your risks:

Step 1 - Figure out the maximum dollar risk for the trade you are planning

Take note that this should not be higher than the 2% of your account. Make sure that you have calculated this before you start your trading day.

For example, let's say that you have a $20,000 account. With the 2% rule, you can only risk $400 for a single trade. If you want to be more conservative, you can limit yourself to trading $200 every trade or 1% of your account.

Step 2 - Estimate your max risk per share and stop-loss strategy

Let's say that you are looking at the stock of BBRY (Blackberry) using ABCD Pattern Strategy. You buy stocks at $8 and want to sell it at $11, with a stop loss at $6.50. You will be risking $1.50 / share.

Step 3 - Find the absolute maximum number of shares you should trade each time

You can do this by dividing 1 by 2. Following the examples above, you will be allowed to buy only 133 shares or rounded to 125 shares.

You can only consider max loss for your account depending on your account size. So you need to make that call for yourself. For instance, if your stop is higher than your moving average, you need to make some calculations and check if this stop is bigger than the maximum account size.

If the break of moving average will yield a $300 loss, and you have set a $200 max loss every trade, then you must cancel the trade or take a lower number of shares.

You may think that it can be difficult to compute share size or stop loss depending on a max loss on your account, while you are waiting for the right opportunity. It's true that you need to make fast decisions or you may lose the opportunity. It is also true that computing your stop loss and max loss in your account size in a live trade is not usually easy.

Let me take you back to Rule No. 2: Day Trading Is Hard.

You need to practice, and it is ideal for amateur traders to practice under supervision for at least three months in a simulated account. Through this, you can learn how to manage your account as well as your risk for every trade. Gradually, you can easily figure out the numbers by yourself.

Risk Management and Trading Psychology

Day trading is often difficult and a lot of new traders fail. It requires sound decision-making skills, as well as strong self-discipline.

When you learned that an investor has taken a stake in Tesla, your initial reaction might be to join the trend. However, you need to make a fast decision whether you must buy or sell or sell short Tesla stocks. You can effectively do this with discipline.

Your trading strategies will gradually improve over time. But as early as now, you should understand that the key to making money in day trading is to control yourself, and practice self-discipline.

It can be difficult to predict the stock market behavior, and if you don't know what you will do, you can lose the game.

You need to stand on your own feet as even the most advanced trading tools cannot help a trader who doesn't know what to do. You need to ask the following questions:

- Does this particular course of action fit into my trading strategy?

- What trading strategy will this action fit into?

- If this trade goes awry, where do I stop?

- How much money am I risking in the trade, and what is the potential reward?

This is what many day traders find difficult. The decision-making process in day trading is usually a tough multitasking call. On top of that, you may feel the pressure. Many day traders, even successful ones, still find themselves looking at their screens and can't even figure out what action to take.

This type of paralysis is not uncommon when you are under pressure. When this happens, you must understand that you might have pushed yourself a bit too far out of your comfort zone. It can happen even to the most experienced day trader, albeit only once in a while.

By trading regularly, you will gain some experience, and it's ideal to work on the edge of your comfort zone so you can push your boundaries. But if you find yourself too far outside of your comfort zone and beyond your risk tolerance, you may end up making some costly errors. It is always best to foster a self-awareness.

Learn how to be calm under pressure, so you can make decisions without losing your mind. Regularly assess your decisions and always evaluate your performance.

Are you making profits in your trades? Are you getting winning streaks or losing streaks? If you are losing five trades in a row, are you checking your emotions and maintaining your composure? Or will you let your judgment cloud your mind?

Discipline is crucial to develop your trading muscles, which require exercise to grow. Once you have developed these muscles, you need to exercise regularly so you can maintain your physique.

Day trading can give you this opportunity. Regularly exercise your ability to demonstrate discipline and self-control. Some of these skills are also comparable to learning to drive a car. Once you have acquired this skill, no one can take it away.

When you've learned it, the skill of identifying a great stock chart will not fade away. However, discipline is something that you need to regularly work at to be a profitable trader.

You have chosen a venture in which constant learning is important. This profession can be invigorating. But take note that if you begin to gain too much confidence, and think you have outsmarted the market on trading know-how, or that there is no need to learn anymore, you will surely get a quick reminder from the stock market.

You may lose money, and you shall see that the market can rectify your overconfidence. The ability to make fast decisions and your ability to make and then follow your rules for day trading are important for success in this market.

As you read this guide, you can learn more about risk management.

Everything that you do as a day trader comes back to managing risks because, at the end of the day, this is the most important concept for you to understand.

Visualize yourself as a risk manager. You need to effectively manage risks so that you can make good decisions even under extreme pressure. This leads us to Rule No. 6 in day trading:

Rule No. 6 - Your Broker Will Trade the Stocks for You

Your focus is to manage risk. It can be quite difficult to become a successful day trader without effective risk management skills, even if you are knowledgeable with many trading strategies.

Day traders are in the business of day trading. You must clearly define your risk as a business person. You must specifically know the amount of money you are willing to risk on any single trade.

The acceptable risk depends on the size of your trading account as well as your trading method, personality, as well as risk tolerance. This rule is very important that we need to highlight it again: the maximum amount that you can risk on any trade should not exceed 2% of your account size.

For instance, if you have a $60,000 account, you should not risk more than $1200 per trade. If you have a $20,000 account, you should never risk more than $400 per trade.

If your account is still small, you should limit yourself to trading fewer shares. If you think there's a good trade, but a logical step is to place where more than 2% of your equity is at risk, sit it out and move on. You may have minimal risk, but you should never risk more.

Again, never risk more than 2% of your day trading account.

CHAPTER 6 OPTIONS TRADING

What is an option

An option is simply a contract between two parties which is based on an underlying asset. You can create an options contract for any type of asset, but our focus is on options contracts for stocks. They are called options because one party of the contract will have the option to buy or sell stocks depending on whether or not certain conditions are met.

An option is a type of derivative. While they've been around for a long time, the general public really didn't become aware of the concept of derivatives until the 2008 financial crash, when a particular type of derivative, mortgage-backed securities, caused financial havoc when huge numbers of bets went bad at the same time.

One option contract represents 100 shares of stock. The contract will cost the buyer a much smaller sum than it would cost to buy the shares of stock. In a sense, an options contract is a bet that the stock will move in a certain direction over a given time period. That is why they can be used for speculation.

There are, of course, only two ways a stock can move, and so there are two types of options contracts. These are:

- A call: this is a bet that the stock will rise in price on or before the ending date of the contract.

- A put: this is a bet that the stock will decline in price, on or before the ending date of the contract.

For a call, the condition that the contract is based on is that the price of a share of stock will go up past an agreed upon price per share, which is called the strike price. When it does, the buyer of the option can exercise their right to buy the shares of stock from the seller (or writer as they are called) of the call option. That is, they can "call it in". If the share price goes above the strike price, the

writer or seller of the call contract must sell the shares if the buyer chooses to exercise their right to buy them.

This is true no matter how high the stock price has risen. So, suppose that the strike price for ABC stock was set at $67 when the contract was entered into by the two parties. Second, we'll assume that at that time the share price was $65. If the share price rises to

$68 a share, the owner of the shares must sell them if the buyer wants to exercise their option (to buy the shares). This is also true if the share price rises to $100.

The seller of the contract takes a bit of risk. They can't lose money, but they might miss out on a big move in the share price of the stock, and hence miss out on a big profit they could have had.

Why bother? The reason is that the buyer can buy the shares at the strike price. If the shares have risen to $100 a share, the buyer can buy the shares from the seller of the options contract at $68 per share, and then immediately turn around and sell them for $100 a share, making a quick profit of $32 per share! Of course, that is a quote of gross revenue, there are some fees involved and a commission to the broker, but in the end, the buyer would make a substantial profit in this scenario.

Now you may be wondering why the person selling the contract would bother. The reason is that they can charge a non-refundable fee for entering into the contract. This fee is called the premium. If you're selling calls, you get to keep the premium no matter what. In many cases, the share price will never exceed the strike price, so they get to keep the premium and the shares. In the event that it does exceed the strike price, they get to keep the premium, and even though they may have missed out on some profit they could have had, they will probably earn a bit of profit on the shares they sold anyway. For the seller, it's a win-win deal. This kind of option contract is known as a covered call.

Covered calls provide one option strategy, which is to generate income from your shares.

Premiums are small, as compared to the price of the underlying stock. The risk to the buyer of the call is relatively small, and they get the chance to control shares of stock for a certain time without actually owning them. Of course, to exercise your option, you will have to have the capital on hand or access to the capital in order to buy the shares to make your quick profit. Many people, however, don't even do that and they simply trade options (that is you get the contract, and then sell it on the options markets before the expiry). Options contracts are for 100 shares each. Premiums will usually be pretty small, so say $1 per share, so you can buy the options contract for 100 shares for $100. If it doesn't work out for the buyer, they lose a relatively small amount of money, as compared to the large funds that would be involved actually buying the stock. From the buyer's perspective, it gives them the ability to speculate on the markets for relatively small sums of money and without actually owning the stock. Then if their speculation proves right, they can exercise their options and buy and sell the shares of stock.

When you read about options, they are typically described in some fancy sounding language. It will make sense now that you've seen how a covered call works. For a call, an option is a contract giving the owner the right, but not the obligation, to buy shares of stock at a fixed price over a specific, limited time period. Typically, options contracts last a few months, but you can also buy weeklys, which last a week on Fridays. There are also quarterly which expire the last business day at the end of each quarter. Also, for long term considerations, you can buy LEAPS which is typically a time period over a few years.

Now let's take a look at the other type of options contract, which is known as a put. A put gives the buyer the right to sell the underlying stock at an agreed-upon price on or before the expiration date. Again, the put contract is sold for a premium and the pre-agreed upon share price is known as the strike price. When a trader buys a put, the bet is that the price of the stock will go below the strike price over the lifetime of the contract. Let's illustrate with an example.

Joe buys a put contract for XYZ Company. At the time that he buys the put contract, XYZ is trading at $100 a share. The premium for the contract is $2, so he buys it for $200. The strike price is $90.

Joe believes or has heard that some bad news will come out about XYZ, or maybe he is simply bearish about the market at large. Then before the contract expires, the bad news does come out. The share price drops to $60. Now Joe can exercise his right in the contract. He buys 100 shares on the stock market at $60 a share. The seller of the put contract must buy the shares from Joe – at the strike price. So, the seller buys 100 shares of XYZ stock at $90 a share, and Joe walks away with a $30 per share profit (less the premium fee and brokerage commission).

The seller of the put got a raw deal, they probably doubted the news would drive the stock price that low, and so made a bet it wouldn't in order to get the income from the premium. Even though they lost their bet they get to keep the premium, so they aren't totally out.

They also have the 100 shares of XYZ, and who knows, maybe things will turn around in the future.

These are dramatic examples designed for illustration. Most of the time stock probably won't move that much, although options traders try to look for volatile stocks that are moving a lot. Sellers will probably try and sell more stable stocks, so they won't risk as much.

If the share price of stock never goes above the strike price in the case of a call or goes below the share price in the case of a put by the expiration date, the option expires worthless. The seller of the option walks away with their premium and in the case of the call, keeps their shares, and in the case of a put, has no obligation to buy shares. The buyer of the option loses only the premium when the option expires worthless (note that the buyer never gets the premium back under any circumstances).

Trading Options

Now like anything else, you can buy and sell an option itself. What is an option worth? The premium! Depending on various factors, the premium can go up or down. The person who buys the options contract is the owner of the contract. The seller still has their obligation, if the share price meets the required conditions against the strike price in the contract.

The owner of the option is considered to be long in the position. If you are short on the position, that means you've sold an option you didn't own at the time of sale.

The buyer of an option has three possible outcomes:

- They can hold the option until it expires, and the strike price is not exceeded, so the option expires worthless.

- They can sell the option at some point before it expires. In this case, you are said to "close out your position".

- They can exercise their rights under the option. This means you will buy the underlying shares of stock or sell the underlying shares of stock, for a call or a put, respectively.

The buyer of the option is the person with the right but not the obligation to buy or sell the shares. The seller of the option contract (also sometimes called the writer) has an obligation to buy or sell the shares. Their possible outcomes are:

- You can buy the option back and close out your position.

- Take "assignment", which means buy or sell the shares as required if they have met the condition set by the strike price.

- If the strike price condition isn't met, you let the contract expire worthlessly, and keep your premium.

Of course, remember that in all cases the seller always keeps the original premium.

An option can be in the money or out of the money. If an option for ABC stock has a strike price of $50 and shares of ABC stock are trading for $55, the option is in the money $5. If the shares are trading for $47, the option is out of the money $3.

For a call, it works in the opposite way, since you earn money as the buyer of the option if the stock falls below the strike price. For ABC, a put option with a strike price of $50, if the stock price is trading at $55, the option is out of the money $5. On the other hand, for a put contract, if it's trading at $40, the option contract is in the money $10.

The intrinsic value of an option is the amount that it is in the money. We also need to know the so-called time value of the option. This is the difference between the intrinsic value and the premium per share paid for the option. That is:

Time value = premium paid – value in the money

If you paid $7 for an XYZ option and it's in the money $2, the time value is $7 - $2 = $5.

When an option is out of the money, it has no intrinsic value. So the time value is given by the premium paid, but it declines at increasing rates as the expiration date gets closer. In other words, the options contract will be worth less and less to a potential buyer since its likely to expire worthlessly.

When you look at an options ticker, it will include the premium (the cost of buying on a per share basis) and the expiration date. Options also have a deliverable, which is the amount of the underlying that will be bought or sold if the option is exercised. Typically, this is 100 shares of the stock. The multiplier defines the net credit or debit to your account if the option is exercised (or assigned, in the case that you are the writer of the option).

A few more things to be aware of as a buyer include:

- Break-even point: This is the strike price + option premium.

  - Maximum loss: Premium paid for the option. Long vs. Short

There are four basic options available:

- Long call: this is the right to buy shares. An example would be buying a covered call option as described earlier. This means you are bullish on the stock, that is you expect its value to increase, possibly by a large amount.

- Long put: this is the right to sell shares of stock. You're bearish on the stock, but it's long because you expect to

  profit from the options contract by being able to sell the shares at the strike price which is higher than the share price on the market.

- Short call: An obligation to sell a stock. You're bearish on the stock, and don't believe the share price will increase enough to beat the strike price. It can be covered, meaning that you already own the shares (lower risk) or naked, which means you don't own the shares when you write the contract (high-risk trade).

- Short put: This is an obligation to buy shares of stock. You're bullish on the stock and believe the share price will stay above the strike price.

Now let's size up potential profits and losses for the different options.

Long Call (role: buyer)

For our long call, let's assume we have:

Long 1 ABC Aug 50 Call @ $1

This means the option contract is for 100 shares (the value 1 = 100 shares, or one option contract) of ABC stock. The option expires the third Friday in August. The strike price is $50, and the premium is

$1. This is a low-risk strategy with your only risk limited to the premium, with high potential upside (thought the probability of going above the strike price may not be high). It's also low risk for the seller since they keep the premium and the worst case outcome is selling the shares at the strike price which was higher than the price of the shares at the time the contract was written, but lower than the market price at the time of sale.

For the buyer of this contract:

- The maximum loss is limited to the premium, which is the quoted price multiplied by 100 for the total number of shares, or $1 x 100 = $100.
- Maximum gain: Theoretically unlimited, depending on how much the share price exceeds the strike price.

Short or Naked Calls (role: seller)

We began our discussion with covered calls. In that case, as the seller of the option, the call was "covered" by the underlying stock.

A naked call is one that is uncovered. That is, you write call options without owning the underlying stock. Remember for a call option, if you are forced into an assignment, you must sell the underlying shares. With a naked call, you face potential losses since you don't own the shares when you write the call. On the market, naked calls are known as "shorts". The ticker might look something like this:

Short 1 ABC Jun 25 Call @ $2

This tells us that the option contract expires the third Friday in June. The strike price is $25, and the premium is $2. In this case:

- The breakeven point is strike price + option premium = $25 + $2 = $27.
- Maximum gain is 100 shares x premium = $200.
- Maximum loss is unlimited, depending on how high the stock goes because you would have to buy the shares if assigned. Since this is high risk and you'd need the capital available to take care of the deal if the need arises, brokerages assign levels to options traders to determine whether or not they are allowed to participate in such high-risk trades. When you open an account to trade options, you'll need to know what your assigned level is to determine which types of trades you can make.

Short Puts (role: seller)

A short put, like a naked call, is a risky trading strategy and you'll be required to have capital available to risk. This is a small possible gain with a large possible loss option. Consider the following put:

Short 1 ABC Jul 30 Put @ $2

This option expires the third Friday in July, has a strike price of $30 and a premium of $2.

- Maximum gain: $2 premium x 100 shares = $200.
- Maximum loss: ($30 strike price - $2 premium) x 100 = $2,800.
    - Break-even: ($30 strike price - $2 premium) = $28.

Long Put (role: buyer)

For a long put, we're betting that the stock price is going to drop below the strike price. This is a lower risk strategy than a short put for the buyer. If the price fails to drop below the strike price, then you're only out the premium. Of course, to exercise your right to sell the shares, you'll have to have access to the capital necessary to buy them.

CHAPTER 7 HOW DOES FOREX WORK?

Just like the stock markets, one can trade currencies depending on his/her prediction on the changes of value. The greatest difference between stocks and currency trades is that forex can trade down and up very easily. If one thinks that a particular currency will have a value increase, he/she may buy it, and if he thinks that the currency will fall, he /she may sell it. The forex market is so large that finding a buyer or seller is too easy compared to other trade markets. Let's assume that a trader hears reports that a country such as China will devalue its currency with the intention of drawing more foreign investors into the country. If he/she thinks that the devaluing trend will continue, the trader may sell the currency of China against another, for example, the USD. The more the currency of China devalues against the United States dollar, the higher the trader's profit. However, if the currency gains value against the US dollar,

then the trader will have increased losses and may want to leave the trade as soon as possible.

Summarily, Forex trading involves placing a bet on the value of one currency against the other. Remember that in a pair, the first currency is the base while the second currency is the secondary or the counter. This means that if a forex trader thinks that the EUR will increase in value in contrast with the United States dollar, he/she will buy the EURUSD. If the trader thinks that it will drop, he/she will sell the EURUSD. If for instance the asking price 0.7060 and the bid price is 0.7064, and then the spread price is 4 pips. Whether the value of the EUR rises or falls, the trader will make a profit or loss once he covers the spread price. The spread price is usually higher for minor currencies.

CONCLUSION

After learning everything that you could ever possibly want to know on how to pull off a marketing campaign on Instagram, there is still one question that you need to answer:

Is marketing on Instagram all worth it?

This does not ask if the platform is the right fit for your business as that is something that you should answer yourself. What it does ask, however, is if there is a point to even trying to venture into Instagram.

When it comes to Instagram, there are always 4 points that you have to consider in determining if the platform is the right channel to do your marketing in.

Stories Matter now More than Ever

The launch of Instagram stories and other similar features in social media sites have proved one thing for marketers: you can no longer sell anything online just with pretty pictures or quotable text.

Stories have a highly interactive and multimedia nature in them which means that they can be consumed in various ways (even ways that you did not plan for) and encourage people to engage with the, driving traffic up to a considerable degree. And if people are engaged, they retain information at a far better rate.

Everyone Is Into Collaborating

CPSIA information can be obtained
at www.ICGtesting.com
Printed in the USA
BVHW091116120521
607049BV00008B/2182